Being Number One
At
Being Number Two

Understanding
Another Man's Vision

Cornell King

Table of Contents

Forward

Being Number One at being Number Two "Understanding Another Man's Vision", is an impressive and moving work that is much needed in the Church today. This work was designed for those individuals who have been gifted and called as *leaders* to minister alongside their Pastors. It is an easy read for everyone that may find themselves in the position of serving as an assistant pastor or ministry leader and is seeking to better understand their role within their respective ministry. It will shed light on how leaders may learn and discern what is required of them to effectively serve their Pastor in the capacity for which they have been called.

This work is also geared towards those individuals (leaders/ leaders in training) who are able to accept the challenge of not knowing every detail of every matter and are striving to be the best they can be in the position for which they have been called; in other words (Being Number One at being Number Two). What I hope to accomplish in this writing is to mine biblical nuggets (principles) for the reader; nuggets that you will embrace, utilize and treasure for life. It is my intent to lay down biblical principles that would assist the reader in visualizing and grabbing hold of the hypothesis that you <u>can</u> be Number One at Being Number Two. However, the most important principle in becoming Number One at Being Number Two is that you must first commit to, articulate and fully support the vision of the one that is out front. As the Apostle Paul writes in Philippians 2:5, "Let this mind be in you which was also in Christ Jesus".

One may ask the question, what is this mind?... What is it not? Well... here is what I know and believe. It was, is and will always be a mind of humility... a mind of obsequiousness, a mind of servant-hood, a mind of obedience and total subjection to the will of God. It was not and is not a carnal or natural mind that can be tossed to and fro by the tenants of this world.

In essence it is a Spiritual mind originating in the heart of God. Now then, let us understand that we (the saints of God) have the Mind of Christ, and the Spirit of Christ. With that understanding and with our faith, we can start to operate in that revelation. Then we will see that it is not difficult at all to serve, support and understand "Another Man's Vision."

Proverbs: 27:17-18
17 "As iron sharpens iron; so a man sharpens the countenance of his friend.
18 "Whoever keeps the fig tree will eat its fruit; so he who waits on his master will be honored."

Proverbs helps us understand (vs. 17) the advantages of good conversation. It is profitable to each person and the one with greater knowledge will impart that knowledge to the other/s. This kind of discourse with a friend/s will help to sharpen one's wits (iron sharpening iron) and each gains wisdom and pleasure from it. The countenance of a friend is the company of, or the conversation with a friend that yields pleasure and builds strong relationship/s. In vs. 18 we are to understand that we are not to be discouraged by our calling;

for like the fig tree our calling in ministry is labor intensive and requires much care, attention and diligence. Sometimes the labor is so laborious that we may start to question or even dislike it. This is true for all leaders, but especially for those leaders who are serving their Pastors. We are charged with being careful observers so that we may learn and absorb all that vs. 18 our master has to impart to us. We must be obedient and do all that we can to safeguard their health and well being as well as their reputation and the financial and spiritual health of the Church. Daunting…yet vs. 18 tells us that if we do not faint; if we are diligent, steadfast, and resolute; and if we persevere, serve faithfully and prudently, we shall be honored, have preference and be rewarded. Simply put…the manner in which we serve, so shall we also be served.

Deuteronomy 4:6
"Therefore, be careful to observe them (the commandments) for this is your wisdom and your understanding in the sight of the peoples who will hear all these statutes…

The fact is there are many biblical principles and commandments from the heart of God that are simply awaiting our application. In the book of Deuteronomy we are told that when we allow these principles or commandments to govern our lives, then we will know our position, we will be the best in it, and we will serve with the full knowledge in all that we do, we are laying up for ourselves a good foundation.

Introduction

I want to start by saying I am more than thankful that God has chosen me to be a vessel and a mouthpiece to get this information out. I have fasted and consecrated myself that I may hear from Him. You see, it wasn't my idea to write the book. I was inspired by the Holy Spirit to write so I must rely on the Holy Spirit to put it into words that it may be plain to the readers, so they may be able to understand and run with it. The sub-title of this book is: "Understanding Another Man's Vision."

Proverbs 4:7 tells us that,
"wisdom is the principal thing; Therefore get wisdom. And in all your getting, get understanding."

This work will address the topics of loyalty, and humility, and it will deal with the rewards and benefits of being number one at being number two. Additionally, it will also give insight and direction to leaders in understanding your responsibilities in serving and building a competent, ethical, discerning and most of all spiritual relationship with your Pastor.

In helping you to understand relationships and positioning, there are three Biblical relationships that we will look at; Joshua and Moses, Paul and Timothy and Elijah and Elisha. In each of these relationships, there is a lesson to be learned. Leaders that are in a number two position at some point would find themselves experiencing one or more of these relationships. But have no fear, this is a healthy thing. The key is to be able to identify where you are in the relationship with your Pastor and to adjust accordingly.

Jesus has given the perfect example of what it's really like to be Number One at being Number Two. I think it is so important that we rely heavily on the example that has already been given us through the life of Jesus Christ. In the fallen world so often we are told that, "to be number two means that you have somehow "missed the mark" you're good... but not quite good enough...you are not the best. What I have come to appreciate is that being the best is not determined by a number or a rating. Being the best is determined by walking in integrity... being the best is determined by being humble, and walking in humility. I have concluded that being the best requires being loyal, and disciplined which will produce character... for these are the main ingredients in becoming the best that one can be. Being Number One at being Number Two means, as John the Baptist expresses in John 3:30 that, "He (Christ) must increase, but I must decrease"

As leaders, this is the same position we should take with our Pastors. If you are willing to take this position, ask yourself: "what result would there be for someone watching my life and following me? What will they see and where will they end up as a result of watching and following my life? Selah.

The actualization of being number one at being number two was derived from my current position with my Pastor. I understood the scripture better that says, "To whom much is given, much is required." In today's society, it is evident that more often than not, people are driven by titles and positions. All too often ministry leaders bring this secular mindset into the Church and they find it difficult if not impossible to adapt and function in the body of Christ. Leaders must understand and accept the fact that their ministry is a calling that God has placed on their lives. It is not a scenario where we wake up one morning and decide that we want to be in ministry and then a few months later have a change of mind... no, it's not that simple.

As you read I hope that you will take hold to one of the important principles that I hold dear and that is, that the called men and women of God, should walk upright before God, believers, and unbelievers; displaying a faith and confidence that says I am totally dependent upon God for all things.

I hope and pray that this book will be an encourage-ment, and an inspiration to its readers. And for those that may occasionally wonder... why is it that I'm where I am? ...And where do I go from here? I pray that the eyes of your understanding will be enlightened through this work.

Dedication

This book is dedicated to:

Dr. Ronald F. Kimble Sr. – Every man has a purpose in this dispensation of time that we know as life. Pastor, I am grateful that God has given me favor, that you believe in me, instruct me, correct me and encourage me. You have brought me into a realm that few individuals are able to speak about... And that is *Son-ship*... I Thank God for You, and may He continue to richly bless your life.

Acknowledgements

A Special Thanks to my loving and devoted wife Muriel, for loving me and believing in me. You are truly an inspiration to me and I am truly blessed to have you as my wife.

Thank you, Joshua Marquis (my son) for sharing your father and sacrificing our time together.

Thanks to: Prophetess Francina Norman for giving the prophetic birth to this writing. I am grateful to you, for being the vessel God chose to release the spirit within me to begin this journey.

Thanks to: Dr. Christopher J. Esbenson for providing the tools and encouragement to bring this writing to pass. I appreciate your embracing me and giving me the time that was much needed in the success of this writing.

I would like to thank and acknowledge all of you that took part in any way in the success of this writing.

1
Loyalty

Either You Are or You're Not

L oyalty is faithfulness or a devotion to a person or cause. Loyalty is <u>not</u> something that you pick up today and put down tomorrow. Neither is it designed so that you can be loyal in one area of your life and disloyal in another… Either you're loyal or you're not.

This is one of the underlying traits that many Pastors look for as they bring people into their inner circle. A good example of this is our President during the selection of his vice president. The President must choose with great care because this person will be his successor in the event something should happen. Regardless of what Ivy League school the nominee might hail from, I am certain that loyalty and dedication, steadfastness and permanence are some of the traits that will put a nominee in a position of consideration.

The President considers this person's faithfulness and devotion to their family, their country and political party as part of the selection process. Once the selection has been made, the vice president will be entrusted with information pertaining to the working of this country that many would not be privileged to know. Along with this privilege comes dependence and trust that says, "I know you are with me." During the course of this relationship, there are numerous duties that will be entrusted to the number two person, and it becomes their responsibility to make sure that these duties are carried out.

And, so it is with a Pastor when he prepares to select his second in command. The Pastor must choose with great care because this person will possibly be his successor and will be responsible for leading the Church and upholding the legacy left by the Pastor.

The Pastor already has a blueprint for the character of his successor. It is the same blueprint he had to follow and that blueprint is found in 1 Timothy 3:2-7. In verse 2 the Word of God says,

---

"he must be blameless, the husband of one wife, temperate, sober-minded, of good behavior, hospitable and able to teach..."

Regardless of what College or Seminary the nominee might have attended loyalty, commitment, dedication, steadfastness and permanence are just some of the traits that put the nominee in a position of consideration.

---

1 Timothy 3: 4-5 "one who rules his own house well, having his children in subjection with all reverence, (vs.5) for if a man does not know how to rule his own house, how will he take care of the Church of God..."

Once the selection has been made the Senior Pastor will rely on the Assistant Pastor (some Churches have different titles but for this work we will use Assistant Pastor) to represent the Senior Pastor to the people. The Assistant Pastor, as with the

Vice President, will be entrusted with information pertaining to the workings of the Church that others will not be privy to. Likewise, with this privilege comes dependence and trust that says, "I know you are with me, I can depend on you." During the course of this spiritual relationship, there will be numerous duties that will be entrusted to the number two person, and it becomes their responsibility to make sure that these duties are carried out.

I believe this is one of the most difficult areas in many Churches today. Difficult in the sense that (if leaders, who are serving Senior Pastors) are not careful, they will find themselves pursuing popularity as opposed to being faithful and devoted to the one that God has placed them alongside.

It is so easy to get caught up in opinion polls and what I call Parking Lot Ministry (PLM). Here is an example of PLM. Your Pastor has given you an opportunity to stand before the people; the next thing he hears is that you are trying to start your own ministry. No, there is nothing wrong with a leader starting his/her own Ministry...if that is what God has called you to do. The real problem is that you are attempting to start your ministry with the people God has assigned to your Pastor, the very one whom you are called to safeguard.

We know that "God is not the author of confusion", so why would anyone think that God would want them to steal sheep from the flock? That is not of God! Yet we see it happens time and time again.

Let's understand two very important facts about PLM. 1: It is perverted and demonic; 2: It carries the same seducing spirit that Satan attempted to use with Jesus in the wilderness. After Jesus had fasted forty days, Satan tried to get him to give up his loyalty to the Father. Jesus didn't fall for it and neither should we.

Quite often we do not understand that we really don't understand...

You see, I don't think that we "understand what we don't understand". I know this statement may sound somewhat like an oxymoron, but it seems to be the truth in many cases. When Leaders feel they are not the Leader/Pastor in the church, they have a tendency not to see anything wrong with what is going on around them in the Church body. Unfortunately, some leaders see things in light of the way they *feel in their hearts*..."well it's not really my responsibility; this really isn't my Church; let the Pastor deal with it, I'm just going to focus on what I can do and leave the rest for someone else; I don't get the credit for it anyway so why bother"?

Did I not say earlier that PLM is demonic and perverted? Demonic to the extent that anytime something is said or done contrary to the Word of God or His representative it can be viewed as demonic. It is quite often very difficult for leaders to set aside their own views and take up the views of the one that is out front. But that is what Jesus did and that is what we, as leaders, are required to do.

Every sheepfold has a Shepherd. Likewise, every Church has its Pastor and he or she is the one that God has given the vision for the people to follow. There can only be one visionary in each Church. To have two visions going at the same time, would be to go against Scripture, shows disobedience, is insubordinate and will result in confusion, dissention and division in Church leadership and the body itself will suffer.

We, as leaders must remember that it is God's purpose and God's will that we assist in caring for His people. To that end, Leaders must first understand that they must be trustworthy in order to be trusted. You must be completely loyal to the visionary/Pastor of your Church. Here is a nugget I hope you will treasure: Loyalty is not what you do in the presence of your leader or Pastor, it is what you do (and say) when you are not in their presence.

Loyalty is not what you do in the presence of your leader or Pastor, it is what you do (and say) when you are not in their presence.

I am grateful that I've learned over the years of working closely with my Pastor, that I am growing... I have grown ... and I will continue to grow. As I grow, I am directed by my faithfulness and kept by my devotion and obedience to God and to my Pastor.

When leaders understand that God rewards loyalty and honesty, then we are not so easily moved when people come to us with their views and opinion as to what the Church or Pastor should be doing or where they think the Church should be. Church people will encourage you to believe that you are ready to launch out and start your own Church. However, wisdom would have you to understand that your destiny is tied up in the loins of your Pastor. I clearly understand that no one can release me to do anything for the body of Christ except my Pastor. This is order in the Kingdom. Unless my Pastor releases me, I am out of order.

I believe that God will speak to the one He has assigned you to with regards to your direction and movement.

For My thoughts are not your thoughts; nor are your ways My ways," says they Lord. Isaiah 55:8

Let's not lose sight of how some of us as leaders, ended up as assistants to Pastors. I cannot speak for you, but if your Pastor is like mine, God had to speak to him and let him know whom he should select as his assistant. When God is at the head, it should not be the traditional pecking order that puts you in a position of being number two. God has a wonderful way of doing things that is beyond our comprehension and beyond our understanding. Isaiah 55:8 tells us that our thoughts are not His thoughts and neither are our ways His ways.

I am grateful that God has placed me where I am. Only God knows what He has placed in me and only God will be able to bring it out. From my past experiences, I have come to realize that when God has placed you alongside His servant, being number two requires and even demands a higher degree of discipline. There are even times when God will test you and cause you times of displeasure, discomfort, and anxiety to the point where you may even question God and ask, "God, are you sure this is what You have for me to do?"

When I was going through my testing period, I was reminded of the principle of son-ship that is captured in Hebrews 12:11. Here the Scripture clearly tells us:

"Now no chastening seems to be joyful for the present, but painful; nevertheless, afterward it yields the peaceable fruit of righteousness to those who have been trained by it.

It is loyalty and obedience that keeps you during these times. The gist of the matter here is that you cannot follow, lead, or serve anyone without being loyal.

For I am convinced, that all character traits hinges on Loyalty… And you either you have it…or you don't.

2
Humility

The Beginning of Honor

My experiences have led me to understand that I do not know as much as I think I do. Reality says if I have never been in the position of "Being Number One at Being Number Two" then what precedence is there for me to reference? One of the first things I learned was that the difference in the magnitude of the responsibilities of the Pastor and his assistant are tremendous. I have also come to learn that there is a vast difference between the two positions albeit that we think it's just one position higher than the other.

It is incumbent on leaders to study and understand the differences in the levels of responsibility associated with these positions. That study is a humbling experience and it is my belief that many leaders would conclude that they may no longer be so anxious to step into that Assistant Pastor position after all.

Humility says even though I am not the leader or Pastor, my attitude and my heart should align with his. His concerns become my concerns. I no longer see things through my eyes, but through his. Many times I have found myself juxtaposing my position with that of a young boy who has strong but limited knowledge and understanding of what is really going on around him; yet he is anxious to do what he has seen his father do so many times before.

This young boy finds himself standing in the mist of a crowd of people and not knowing what to do; he suddenly starts clinging to the pant leg of his father and peering around his leg to get a "better" look. The young boy, knows that he is going to have to let go of his father and step out into the crowd by himself, but all too soon he realizes that he really doesn't want to be out front after all. In the mind of this young boy, he concludes that I'm not ready for what my eyes are beholding. I need to stay closer to my father; I need to learn more of his vision; I need more spiritual strength and guidance before I step out. And just like this little boy was humbled, I also am humbled.

This is the reality that humility brings to leaders who really understand or are striving to understand their positioning.

Proverbs 15:33 "The fear of the Lord is the instruction of wisdom, and before honor is humility."

The Bible clearly explains that humility comes before honor. Promotion itself comes from above, *(according to Psalms 75:6-7)* so take heed, and do not allow your position to inflate you and cause you to think that you are someone that you're really not. In other words, you must let the "flesh" die. If you don't keep the flesh in check, you will start down a path that will begin to create dissension and confusion within the Church.

Dissension, which is like a cancer, will spread and eventually lead to death. Dissension, division, and disloyalty are issues that all leaders should be keenly aware of through the unction of the Holy Spirit. Then those leaders must fight with everything in them to keep those spirits from rising up in the Body of Christ. God has charged leaders with the responsibility of accomplishing numerous tasks. And the overarching task is equipping people for the work of ministry.

Whenever you see your Pastor standing before the congregation do you ever think that he is without trials and challenges in his life? Of course we do. But Pastors live in the flesh just like we do and they are not exempt from life challenges. However, our Pastors don't have the luxury that we and many members have. That is, on any given Sunday we may simply say, "Oh today is Sunday, I don't think I want to attend service today; or "I have a headache I'll just stay home today." Our Pastor doesn't have that luxury.

When we understand that the commitment and humility our Pastors display is the modeling for us as assistants and ministry leaders, then, when we are elevated by God into the position of a Pastor, we too will know how to conduct ourselves. We will know how to humble ourselves before the Lord and how to serve the Church with humility and honor.

It is my understanding and belief that God calls no man without first preparing him for the task that they are being called to. No soldier goes to war without the proper training and successful completion of that training which is usually measured by application.

Upon the demonstrated ability of the soldier, he/she is then commissioned and given a set of orders to carry out. So it is in the Kingdom of God. Upon our demonstrated ability to humble ourselves and bring honor to our King Jesus and ourselves then we will receive our commission. For it is through humility that honor comes.

In the next few chapters I will touch on the importance of following your leader. But even more valuable, are the various stages of training that are necessary for leaders to successfully complete. It is through the successful completion of these training stages that God is glorified as we exemplify humility through our lives.

3
Who Are You Following?
...and Who's Following You

God has placed us out front as leaders, to be an example before the people. But, to be a good example we have to understand the pattern that has already been established in heaven for us to follow. Case and point, God told Moses in the building of the Tabernacle, to build it after the pattern that had already been established in heaven.

I am grateful and appreciative that God, from the foundation of the world, chose me to walk along-side my Pastor. The pattern for our relationship has already been established in heaven. It is a relationship where I have not only been mentored but, I have been coached and more importantly "fathered". I strongly believe that patterns are crucial and necessary in the development of leaders who believe they have been called to be number one at being number two.

When you have been commissioned by God to be an assistant to a Pastor, you must first understand that He has placed a mentor, a leader, and an earthly spiritual father, in your life. Clearly, we are intelligent beings who feel that through our own experiences and situations in life, we have gained a measure or level of understanding of how situations, relationships, issues and conflicts play out. But when it comes to the Kingdom of God it is no longer what you know. God will place a person (Pastor) in your life who will be a leader, a mentor and an earthly spiritual father. This person will deposit the Word into you so that you may see things in light of the way that He (God) wants you to see them. It's not business as usual and it's not about you and what you know or think you know. It's about grabbing hold of and understanding another man's vision.

How do you know when God has placed the right leader over you? How do you know when you're the right assistant for that leader? You will know because that relationship will go from one that is generated or initiated by a position, to one that becomes relational even to the point of son-ship.

By son-ship I mean that it's the same that God has with His son Jesus. Furthermore, to truly understand another man's vision is not something that is given to every person. It takes a very unique, gifted and principled individual with a desire to serve rather than to be served, to "understand another man's vision."

Many times we think we know how to approach a matter and for the most part we do. But we approach it based on what we know from previous experiences. The uniqueness of serving someone in the Kingdom is based on the laying down of your will and your desires and taking up that of another... as directed by God. In other words, it comes down to the directive found in

---

Romans 12:1b ..."That you present your bodies as a living sacrifice, holy, acceptable to God, which is your reasonable service."

That sacrifice simply put is... not my will, but the will of the one that I am serving. The uniqueness of this is that while you might know how to approach a matter a certain way or in a particular manner, it is not the only way or approach.

God does not use the same strategy every time and neither should we.

I left a very successful secular position and entered into the Church to serve the Chief Servant of God, my Pastor. I found it to be a whole new world. When you come into the Church on a full time basis, you will find that you must operate on a different set of principles. Working in the secular world is a balancing act. We daily strive to follow the worldly rules and still adhere to our Christianity. But in the Church, we operate solely on Kingdom principles and the difference can be startling.

A kingdom principle, in its simplest meaning says, it is not what you know; but, this is the way God designed it and this is how it is to be done. In essence, it is the Pastor who has the view ...he has the vision ... he's the one that God has placed out front and he's the one to whom God has given the big picture.

Our role as Assistant Pastors and Ministry Leaders is to ensure that everything that the Pastor needs for the success of every endeavor is in place.

Here's what I mean. As the visionary ...as the leader, the Pastor has already determined where we (the Church) is going. So, my role now is to fully understand what the Pastor wants and how he wants to accomplish it. Then, I must make sure we have all that we need to make it happen.

Now, let's say that from my past experience I know another way to accomplish this particular task. Now, my Pastor has stated that we're going to go do it one way and I begin to entertain other possibilities. Leaders, assistant Pastors let me make this very clear to you...that is not my role and it's not yours either. Every leader ought to always remember and consider one very important fact... that is, that God did not give you the command, nor did He give you the vision.

Our role is one of making sure that all the appropriate resources needed to accomplish the Pastors assignment are in place and accounted for. As an example, let us say we are on a safari in the jungle. Since we're in the jungle we know that a machete is one of the most needful tools, so we want to make sure we have machetes as well as sharpening tools to hone the machetes along the way. Also, we want to make sure we have plenty of water, bandages, food, or anything else that we may need supply wise to get to where the leader has been instructed and given the vision to go. Get the picture?

The Pastor's role is to point out the direction. Our position as ministry leaders and assistants is to make sure we are always in constant view of the Pastor and of the direction in which he is guiding us and moving towards. As a result, success is inevitable. I find that this very simple safari analogy is one that is difficult for many ministry leaders and congregants to actually follow. Why? Because we want to use the knowledge we have; we want to impress our leader that we can do things our way and still get the job done.

While that is what we are taught in the secular world, and it might work well there, it does NOT work in the Church. In the Church we follow Kingdom principles and we all know that the Kingdom of God is about "Order". Everything must be done decently and in order. Where much is given, much is required. The accountability for the success of the Church and its body does not rest with the second in command, but with the one who is in command. When God spoke to Moses, He didn't speak to all the Children of Israel, it was Moses that God used for His mouthpiece. And this is the principle that we have to apply and govern ourselves by.

It seems most difficult for believers of Christ to understand this principle. Yes, you have the Spirit of God; Yes, God speaks to you; but when a matter pertains to the Body of Christ, the local Church in particular, God speaks to the one He has placed as Shepherd of that flock. Therefore, it behooves us to come alongside and embrace the Pastor that

32

is out front. Even when we do not understand, or though it was not our idea, we have to follow.

Remember what I stated earlier in the forward? Our role as leaders is first and foremost to commit to, articulate, and fully support the vision of the one that is out front... our Pastor. Secondly, we are to be obedient and do all that we can to safeguard our Pastor's reputation, health and well being, while guarding prayerfully, the financial and spiritual health of the Church. Hopefully, as we faithfully carry out our roles, there are others following our lead. It is a sad indictment to be in leadership and believe that you are a good leader, only to look behind and see there is no one following. We are called and commissioned by God to lead by example just like Jesus did. Therefore, every leader must always be an extension of the one that you are following.

4
The Role of the Servant

What is a servant? In its most basic meaning, a servant is one who is willing to subject himself to another without being in bondage. Every one of us should find ourselves in a servant role. To truly appreciate servant-hood, we first have to understand the principles that were set forth in the relationship with Moses and Joshua.

Joshua did not think it was important that he build a name for himself...

This statement is so vital to the success of leaders it's worth repeating over and over again until it gets into the marrow of your bones. Joshua did not think it was important that he build a name for himself. Today, many people will have you think it's not good enough to be identified or associated with your Pastors name. They would have you believe that you have to make a name for yourself. Not so! It is your Pastor's name that will bring about your identity and make others aware of you. It is his name that will give creditability to the things we put our hands to do. Even our society understands this when it comes to credit. Because they don't know you, they have to take the word of someone else that has had previous experiences with you and the way you handle your obligation with them. If we could ever grasp the importance of the credibility that comes from serving, we will find ourselves accomplishing more than we could ever imagine.

Now, as for Joshua, he saw the importance of serving the man of God both in the good times and in the bad times. Joshua had the opportunity to see a side of the man of God that many people never got the opportunity to see; and such will be (or is) the case for many of us. Like Joshua, we have been privileged to see a side of our Pastors that the average person or Church member would never, ever get exposed to. We are privileged to see the whole man; the human side and the spiritual side, the good days and the bad days, the times of anger, the times of laughter and the times of tears.

We are blessed to know their weaknesses and their strengths. In essence, we see the total humanity of God's anointed one. Our Pastors are not invincible. They simply display their higher degree of trust and faith in God that should challenge us to acquire the same. They display what I call the Joshua spirit.

Have you ever stopped and asked yourself the question, what made Joshua such a good leader? Well, I have, and here's what I have surmised from my research. Joshua was a good leader because he was a good *servant*. He was a faithful servant to Moses and to the people. Joshua was also a military commander. He was a man who both understood and was comfortable with taking and giving orders. Joshua displayed the servant characteristic of a leader who was *number one at being number two*; and he did this by humbling himself, serving his leader and by grasping and taking ownership of "another man's vision."

It was required of Joshua to be exposed to every aspect of Moses humanity and his walk with God, because of the task that God was preparing him for.

Likewise, we too must get as much exposure to, and experience with the one that God has assigned us to, so that we may be prepared to do all that God will place before us. After years of serving Moses, the day came when God told Joshua,

> *"Moses my servant is dead. Now therefore arise and go over this Jordan, you and all this people, to the land which I am giving to them – the children of Israel." (Joshua 1:2)*

God's confidence in Joshua was the result of his faithful servanthood to Moses.

The foundation of anything that God will do in our lives will be predicated on our passion and willingness to serve God by serving those who are in authority over us. Authority is a word that is understood by all true servants. While many people want authority (especially in the Church), not many are willing or able to submit to it nor are they willing to be accountable for the responsibilities that comes with it.

After the announcement of Moses death, God told Joshua to be strong and courageous. God knew then, and He knows now that the people, (the body of Christ), will always need a strong and courageous leader; a leader whose heart, mind and soul are squarely and immovably fixed on God.

Our Pastors endure the same hardships, the same trials, the same tribulations as we do, but they always, (and it's not an option for a good leader) have to exemplify courage, and strength before the people of God, just as our Biblical patriarchs have done throughout history.

When we look at the men and women that we serve and how they stand strong and immovable in the midst of adversity, trials and their disappointments, we recognize the true and Godly stature of our leaders. At the same time, we start to realize that the majority of the people whom our Pastors serve have very little understanding of what these anointed and appointed men and women of God truly endure.

Those of us who are Assistant Pastors have been graced by God to come alongside our Pastors and have been given the opportunity to learn from our Pastors what it means to be a servant of God and a Shepherd of the people of God. We also have been given the awesome task of learning and understanding how to be faithful and humble servants to our Pastors.

Our calling in ministry is labor intensive and requires much care, attention and diligence. Sometimes the task is so laborious that we may start to question or even dislike it. This is true for all leaders, but especially for those leaders who are serving their Pastors as their assistants. We are charged with being careful observers so that we may learn and absorb all that our Pastor has to impart to us. We must be obedient and do all that we can to safeguard their health and well being as well as their reputation and the financial and spiritual health of the Church.

Daunting… yes, but remember earlier when we looked at Proverbs 27:18? Verse 18 tells us that if we do not faint; if we are diligent, steadfast, and resolute; and if we persevere, *serve* faithfully and prudently, we shall be honored, have preference and be rewarded. Simply put…the manner in which we serve, so shall we also be served. Although our days are full and may take us to and fro we need to be mindful of the fact that: sometimes our service to our Pastors will come in the form of being a good listener; sometimes its saying, "please allow me to take on this matter" or "let me relieve you of this burden." I am your servant…

And this is the understanding that we should have…we are required to be servants to our leaders in order to move into the next phase of our journey. What we have discussed thus far is the serving phase where you give and you give… and you give and you give… and then you give - and after you have given, you give some more. All of this giving is because you know, you understand and you believe by faith, that God has an expected end for your life.

Understanding the role of the servant is about seeing how you become the number one servant to the people. In serving the people of God, it is crucial that you keep them before God. You don't cause people to see you, but to see God. And when we can grasp the fact that we are merely sign posts, pointing people to Jesus then we will not loose heart and feel defeated. When people can see how we carry ourselves... the way we handle our affairs with discretion and how our families are obedient, submissive and unified with us, it gives them hope.

So don't grow weary in doing well, and don't keep a track record of what you do for the men and women of God. All that you do should be for the Glory of God; "for your witness is in heaven." When serving the men and women of God, you do it because you have the heart for God and for the people... you're loyal to them and God has predestined you to serve them.

5
The Role of the Student

There is a principle that is found in the writings of the Apostle Paul where he speaks of his relationship with a young Pastor by the name of Timothy. Paul knew that Timothy was a young man and he instructed Timothy to let no one despise his youth. Many times the people of God will view Assistant Pastors the same way. There may even be times when you will be viewed as someone with no significance and in some cases people may attempt to draw upon you only if they feel it would be advantageous to them.

Paul and Timothy's relationship is very unique and worthy of a closer review. In my opinion, this is the model of a student and teacher relationship. All that we would acquire or all that we would come to know about leadership and about ministry, God has already predestined and placed the men and women of God in our lives to lead us into this understanding.

A good teacher will impart wisdom and help you to understand the complexities of the Church and its members. Good teachers will always stress the importance of being doctrinally sound and theologically correct in your teachings. He or she will help you understand that you are not in your position to be popular or to gain popularity by doing things that are popular among the Churches or among the people.

Also, a good teacher will give you sound instruction in the Word of God so that you understand that God's doctrine does not speak to us about popularity but rather it tells us to remain steadfast and hold fast to sound doctrine regardless of what others are doing. A great Pastor/Leader will instill in you the principle that says, "If what is popular cannot be found in the Word of God it is NOT of God; therefore do what God says and NOT what the people say. Good teachers will always emphasis to their student the foundation of his purpose and calling. And, that is that you teach the Word of God. You teach the Word of God in season and out of season; for it is God's Word that is able to bring life. It is God's Word that is able to make the difference and change lives.

As a student you must understand the importance of reading... and reading... and studying and reading.

2Timothy 2:15 (KJV) says, "Study to show thyself approved unto God a workman that needs not be ashamed, rightly dividing the word of truth."

Now, expect your Teacher to drive home this point on a consistent basis. As a good student you are to be obedient to God and to your Teacher by feasting on, and digesting the word until it gets into the marrow of your bones.

A key factor in the student teacher relationship (phase two) is that of fellowship. The fellowship factor is about spending time with your Pastor. Seize every opportunity to be with the man or woman of God because it is an honor to sit and listen at the footstool of your Pastor. It is during these priceless times that you are able to draw on their wisdom and knowledge, and gleam a clearer understanding of the Scriptures. Also, this is the place to ask those questions that you can't ask on Sunday morning. Also, this lend opportunity to ask about words that you really don't know nor understand the content or context of its usage.

These are also the times when we are able to make social observations that at times may be somewhat perplexing. We get an opportunity to draw upon the experiences of our Pastors in handling difficult situations within the body as well as an understanding of how they have dealt with all of the different behaviors of the members.

Understand that the Pastor you are serving has been appointed to do more than just receive your service. He or she has been required of the Lord to nurture, teach, correct, instruct, mentor and guide you as part of their servant-hood to God. They are required by God to speak into your life, to give you instructions, to open your eyes so that your understanding may be enlightened about the crucial matters and issues of ministry and principles that are important to your success in your ministry calling.

It is during this student phase also that we understand through our teachers, that it's not just about the preaching and the teaching that is before the people, it's our whole life. This is a foundational principle for all leaders. As the Apostle Paul says,

---

"we are walking epistles, we are being read daily by everyone that look upon us."

Therefore, since we have been selected and are now students, it is critical that we maintain our lives inside and outside of the Body according to the pattern/blueprint God has given us. Our children have to be obedient, our wives have to be reverent, not slanderers, temperate, and faithful in all things. In essence, we should have our affairs in order inside and outside the Church. Anyone should be able to make an inquiry about our credit-ability. The way we respond to our obligations and handle our personal business outside of the Church is a strong reflection of how we will handle things inside the Church.

So, we see our whole life, our relationships, our behavior, it all matters. Eventually, you will come to realize that your Pastor is there for your spiritual and personal development so that you may be a student that is fully taught and learned in the matters of doctrine; in the matters of the Church and its members, and in the matters of how you live your life. For the Bible declares that: *"when you are fully taught, then you will be as your teacher."*

6
The Becoming of a Successor

The Elijah and Elisha relationship is phase three. Phase three is the successor phase. This is the point in which the man or woman of God, that you have served and have been a student to, now by the grace of God understands that it is time for them to focus on their successor. This is required so that they can move on and accomplish greater works that God is calling them to.

I am so thankful to my Pastor for I have been truly blessed to be along side him. For the past four (4) years I have been under the tutelage of my Pastor with a clear understanding that I would not be put before the people until he said it was time to go before them. In the early part of 2006 my Pastor set me before the congregation and openly acknowledged that I am to be his successor. What an awesome and stunning moment that was.

I am so humbled because God has brought me from out of the depths of hell and set my feet upon a Rock that shall not be moved. When I look back on where I have come from I can only fall on my face and thank Him for His unmerited favor and Grace upon my life.

In that instant I realized that as a successor, you are not just standing on the number of years that you've been serving in ministry or the amount of time you have been a student. Reality hits you square in the face and you realize that you are now standing on the *legacy* that your Pastor has successfully built and is preparing to hand over to you. (Selah)

You are standing in an awe inspiring position of Trust in which the mantle of the "Shepherd" is about to be placed onto your shoulders. You are honored and yet humbled beyond measure before God and all His people. How great and mighty is our God. He knows our end from the beginning. Now the story doesn't end here.

As a matter of fact this is where it really begins and where all of you who are in my position or are waiting placement, should take heed.

When the announcement was made, I could see the response of the people and to me it was overwhelming. You just never know where the people are, but at the same time you can't be so naïve as to think that everyone is for you. What you have to do is hold on to the word of God and to the words of your teacher; "when/if God is for you, who can be against you?

You (leaders in waiting) have to take this nugget and feast on it because we're dealing with flesh, with people; and everyone will not always have your best interest at heart. I thank God for my Pastor because he has helped me to understand that you will find yourself in different seasons. There will be seasons where you will be popular; seasons where you'll feel like you're all alone; seasons where it will seem like nothing is moving or going the way it should, but none of these things should take us by surprise.

Look at our Lord and Savior Jesus Christ: One day the people were saying, "Hosanna, Hosanna, blessed is He who comes in the name of the Lord", and a few days later, these same people, were lifting their voices and saying, "crucify him, crucify him."

So you see we (successors or successors to be) are in a very good position when people turn their backs on us. God has predestined us to do the work of ministry since the beginning of time. And when we understand that having gone through the servant phase and the student phase, all was preparation for phase three, becoming a successor. It is now your time to be number one. You are now ready to succeed your predecessor for he/she has groomed you, prepared you, and they have accomplished what God had placed in their hearts to do so that you can take up the mantle under the anointing of God and their oversight. Your job will be to carry on the legacy and accomplish the work of the Kingdom.

In summary, we have to see ourselves as God see us. We have to understand that it's required of us to walk humbly before those that God has placed over us and given the authority over us. We must understand that many will come to try to sway and pull us away, but our destiny is in the loins of those men and women that God has placed over us, that we should serve them. That we should be a student with – unto them and the end result, if we are obedient, steadfast, humble, loyal and true students of the Word, there will come a time when God will tell them to prepare you to be their successor.

Oh what a day, what a day it was when I look back and all I wanted to do was serve my Pastor, learn as much as I could learn, and honor God with my diligence and obedience. Even now, at the time of this writing, I realize I'm in a position that I've never been in before. But I'm standing with all confidence knowing that the Lord is with me. I stand with the confidence of knowing that my Pastor is with me and is now in the role of coach and mentor as I walk in the Legacy that God has laid out for me. I pray that those of you who are reading this book will understand that you are positioned to become a greater servant unto the Most High God. It is never about us. For, "to whom much is given, much is required."

7
Maintaining Your Balance

One thing that I believe is very important for all individuals in ministry is **balance**.

Balance say, that as you grow and advance you must make sure that you bring your family along with you. As ministry leaders we are to make sure our spouses understand that it is not just the husband or wife walking into this ministry but both of us are literally walking together, for we are one.

Ministry leaders have to be wise enough to know and accept the fact that there will be demands on their time and their family. However, it is crucial to the family unit that we maintain balance even when these demands arise. We must maintain balance with the ministry responsibility God has given us along with our spouses and our children. Let me stop here and say that I also recognize that there are some of us who may have other jobs in the secular world as well, which creates another dynamic in this balancing act. So, let me encourage you by saying that God will not put any more on us than what we can bear. We must, and I can't emphasize it enough, maintain balance in our lives. What good is it for us to do a lot of good works for the church, for the ministry and at the same time, we lose the very thing that God has given us and that is our family?

Proverbs 10:2 "The blessing of the Lord makes one rich and He adds no sorrow with it."

Reflecting back to my first few months in full-time ministry, I was somewhat taken aback by the fact that being in ministry is not like having a nine to five. Many times I would find myself thinking, "Wow, I have a nine to five, and its five o'clock, so let me go home, have dinner with my family, sit down and play with the kids." Sounded good but what I didn't factor in was the understanding that ministry is not just a job, it is a lifestyle.

Yes, it is important to have dinner with the family and play with the children of our inheritance, but we are called to serve as we addressed earlier in our writing. Because of our lifestyles, we are not driven by a schedule that is etched in stone. Our life is not dictated by the clock on the wall, but by the realization of understanding balance.

God has graced each of our lives to be able to deal with the circumstances and the situations that will arise in our lives. After all, He's God! He already knows what is going to come into our lives, and He will give us wisdom as to how to approach every situation - resulting in balance.

A good leader will always appreciate a balanced individual along side him or her in ministry. An individual balanced in the areas of family, fellowship, and their finances. This is so important because these areas are foundational in the lives of all people.

Ministry at times calls for sacrifice. It's when you're able to present yourself a living sacrifice unto God, knowing that this is your reasonable service. Sacrificing to God does not mean that you are to neglect your family. It is so important that you have a balance and many times that balance is misconstrued by people who really don't understand the life you have been called to live. With this said, I want to encourage you to watch out for those individuals that are quick to say, "if I were you." First of all, reality-check here... they are not you. You have to do what God has placed in you to do.

I have found out that as long as you have an understanding spouse, you will be able to maintain balance and be effective in ministry. This is a key point for leaders in any area of ministry, regardless of your position you must have an understanding spouse. You may ask, what is an understanding spouse? An understanding spouse is one whom understands the call that is upon your life by God and embraces it, support it and encourage you with all that is within them.

One other area that deserves our attention in maintaining our balance is communication. It is imperative that we talk with our spouses and get them engaged with the things God is doing in and through our lives. Also, we are to do the same with your children, assuming they are of an age to understand. It is so important that we don't lose sight of family.

The family was designed by God, it was ordained by God and the Church is an extension of our family.

Additionally, balance is necessary when you're alongside a leader that is passionate about what God has given him or her to do. Passionate to the point that you'll find that mediocrity is not acceptable.

There's no room for mediocrity when you have a leader that has the zeal, tenacity and the passion to see all that God has for His people come to pass. In the same manner, there's no way you could walk alongside a true man or woman God and not have them impact your life. Impact is such an operative word here when you understand your position of being number two.

Balance is also synonymous with alignment. The Bible uses the analogy of the oil that ran down Aaron's beard onto his garments. When you are the number two person and you are spiritually aligned with your Pastor, every time the man or woman of God is honored, you are as well due to the trickling down effect which comes directly into your life. Now if you're out of line, then there will be no dimension and no enhancement brought into your life.

I am a staunch believer, (from my own experiences), when you give of yourself it calls for your total being. Not just your intelligence, not just your thoughts and ideas you have to give of yourself entirely. Not to do so would result in you not being able to grasp the vision of your Pastor or Leader.

In conclusion, you have to believe and trust God that it is what He says concerning you that will equip you to maintain a balance while you are in the process of becoming Number One at Being Number Two. Remember that God has already told us all things work together for the good for those of us that love Him and are called according to His purpose.

So, since God has called you and placed you alongside this man or woman of God, then you should give yourself entirely to him or her, knowing that he or she is not going to do anything to bring harm to you. They are not going to tear your family apart... but build it up. They are not going to ask anything that is unreasonable of you...they're not willing to do themselves.

A good Pastor or Leader understands the importance of leading by example. They will show you through their own life that the Word of God is true and the things that they apply to their life, you can apply to yours and it will yield favorable results. I speak very adamantly about this because I've seen it and I am living it out as a result of being with my Pastor whom I love dearly. He is a father to me and he is God-sent. I am of the understanding that I am not assigned to a church (per say), but to a person and for this I am thankful.

I am so blessed that the man whom I look up to as a father, has nurtured me, counseled me, taught me and has equipped me to be Number One at Being Number Two, because God has allowed me to Understand another Man's Vision. Praise God!

8
My Personal Journal

My Journey on Being Number One at Being Number Two

_____

_____

_____

_____

_____

_____

_____

_____

_____

_____

_____

_____

_____

_____

_____

States
639/A